T0084354

"Lay thee down now and rest.
May thy slumbers be blest."

**Johannes Brahms**

# The Lullaby
# Songbook

**WISE PUBLICATIONS**
*part of The Music Sales Group*
London / New York / Paris / Sydney / Copenhagen / Madrid / Tokyo / Berlin

Published by
**WISE PUBLICATIONS**
14-15 Berners Street, London W1T 3LJ,
United Kingdom.

Exclusive Distributors:
**MUSIC SALES LIMITED**
Distribution Centre, Newmarket Road,
Bury St Edmunds, Suffolk IP33 3YB,
United Kingdom.
**MUSIC SALES CORPORATION**
257 Park Avenue South, New York, NY 10010,
United States of America.
**MUSIC SALES PTY LIMITED**
20 Resolution Drive, Caringbah, NSW 2229,
Australia.

Order No. AM993861
ISBN 978-1-84772-582-0
This book © Copyright 2008 Wise Publications,
a division of Music Sales Limited.
Lyrics © Copyright 2008 Dorsey Brothers Limited.
All Rights Reserved.
International Copyright Secured.

Edited by Ann Barkway.
Designed and art directed by Michael Bell Design.
Illustrated by Sonia Canals.
Printed in China.
CD recorded, mixed and mastered by
Jonas Persson.
Backing tracks by John Maul.
Vocals by Rachael Parsons.

Your Guarantee of Quality.
As publishers, we strive to produce every
book to the highest commercial standards.
This book has been carefully designed to
minimise awkward page turns and to make
playing from it a real pleasure.
Throughout, the printing and binding have
been planned to ensure a sturdy, attractive
publication which should give years of enjoyment.
If your copy fails to meet our high standards,
please inform us and we will gladly replace it.

www.musicsales.com

**ALL THE PRETTY LITTLE HORSES...7**
**ALL THE WORLD IS SLEEPING...25**
**ALL THROUGH THE NIGHT...9**
**ARIANA'S LULLABY...5**
**BEDTIME...15**
**BRAHMS'S LULLABY...13**
**BYE, BABY BUNTING...21**
**COVENTRY CAROL...23**
**DANCE TO YOUR DADDY...43**
**EVENING HYMN...51**
**FAR IN THE WOOD...27**
**GAELIC CRADLE SONG...31**
**THE GARTAN MOTHER'S LULLABY...39**
**GO AWAY LITTLE FAIRIES...35**

GOLDEN CRADLE...41
GOLDEN SLUMBERS...47
HEY DIDDLE DIDDLE...49
HUSH-A-BYE, BABY...59
HUSH LITTLE BABY...53
KERRY LULLABY...19
LAMBS ARE SLEEPING...73
LAVENDER'S BLUE...61
LITTLE BO-PEEP...71
LITTLE CHILDREN...77
MANX LULLABY...79
O HUSH THEE, MY BABY...67
ROCK-A-BYE-BABY...89
ROCK THE CRADLE...75
SLEEP ON, LITTLE ONE...83
SLEEP, BABY, SLEEP...85
SLEEP, LITTLE CHILD...87

SLEEPYTIME...91
SWEET AND LOW...93
TEDDY BEAR, TEDDY BEAR...97
TWINKLE, TWINKLE, LITTLE STAR...101
WEE WILLIE WINKIE...99
WINKUM, WINKUM...103

TRACK 1

# ARIANA'S LULLABY

*Ailululu, little baby,*
*Ailululu, kinder.*
*Ailululululu, Ailululululu.*
*Ailululululu, Ailululululu.*

# ALL THE PRETTY LITTLE HORSES

Hushaby, don't you cry,
Go to sleepy little baby.
When you wake you shall have
All the pretty little horses.
Oaks and bays, dapples and greys,
Coach and six of little horses.

# ALL THROUGH THE NIGHT

*Sleep, my child, and peace attend thee,*
*all through the night,*
*Guardian angels God will send thee,*
*all through the night.*
*Soft and drowsy hours are creeping, hill and*
*dale in slumber sleeping,*
*I my loving vigil keeping, all through the night.*

Angels watching ever round thee,
    all through the night,
In thy slumbers close surround thee,
    all through the night.
They should of all fears disarm thee,
    no forebodings should alarm thee,
They will let no peril harm thee,
    all through the night.

While the moon her watch is keeping,
   all through the night,
While the weary world is sleeping,
   all through the night.
O'er thy spirit gently stealing,
   visions of delight revealing,
Breathes a pure and holy feeling,
   all through the night.

# BRAHMS'S LULLABY

*Lullaby, and good night,*
*In the sky stars are bright*
*Round your head, flowers gay,*
*Scent your slumbers till day.*
*Close your eyes now and rest,*
*May these hours be blest,*
*Go to sleep now and rest,*
*May these hours be blest.*

# BEDTIME

The evening is coming,
  The sun sinks to rest,
The crows are all flying straight home
  to the nest.
'Caw,' says the crow as she flies overhead,
'It's time little people were going to bed!'

The butterfly drowsy has folded its wing,
The bees are returning,
     no more the birds sing.
Their labour is over,
     their nestlings are fed,
It's time little people were going to bed.

Goodnight, little people,
      goodnight and goodnight,
Sweet dreams to your eyelids till dawning of light,
The evening has come,
      there's no more to be said,
It's time little people were going to bed.

# KERRY LULLABY

TRACK 6

*Shoheen, sholyoh,*
*the soft shades are creeping,*
*Shoheen my heart's love,*
*the angels are near.*

*Shoheen, sholyoh,*
*my darling is sleeping,*
*Marie's macushla,*
*while mother is near.*

*Hush O, my treasure is dreaming,*
*Lu, la, sleep on till day.*
*Lu-la, miles now are beaming,*
*Shoho, sorrows away.*

*Shoheen, sholyoh,*
*in your white cradle lying,*
*God give you m'leanabh,*
*your night's sweet repose.*

The Lullaby Songbook

19

# BYE, BABY BUNTING

Bye, baby bunting,
Daddy's gone a-hunting.
Gone to get a rabbit skin
To wrap his baby bunting in.

# COVENTRY CAROL

*Lully, lulla, though little tiny child,*
*By by, lully, lullay,*
*Lully, lulla, though little tiny child,*
*By by, lully, lullay.*

# ALL THE WORLD
# IS SLEEPING

Go to sleep upon my breast,
All the world is sleeping.
Till the morning's light you'll rest,
Mother watch is keeping.
Birds and beasts have closed their eyes,
All the world is sleeping.
In the morn the sun will rise,
Mother watch is keeping.

# FAR IN THE WOOD

Far in the wood you'll find a well,
   with water deep and blue,
Whoever drinks by moonlight clear,
Ti-ri, ti-ra, ti-ra-la-la-la,
Will live a thousand years,
   will live a thousand years.

And all around the little well
    are seven lovely trees,
They rock and sway and sing a song,
Ti-ri, ti-ra, ti-ra-la-la-la,
And whisper in the breeze,
    and whisper in the breeze.

And through the seven lovely trees
    the evening wind will blow,
And down fall seven little dreams,
Ti-ri, ti-ra, ti-ra-la-la-la.
My baby all for you, my baby all for you.

# GAELIC CRADLE SONG

*Hush, the waves are rolling in,*
*White with foam, white with foam,*
*Father toils amid the din,*
*But baby sleeps at home, at home.*

Hush the winds roar hoarse and deep,
On they come, on they come.
Brother seeks the lazy sheep,
But baby sleeps at home, at home.

**GAELIC CRADLE SONG**

Hush the rain sweeps o'er the knowes,*
Where they roam, where they roam,
Sister goes to seek the cows,
But baby sleeps at home, at home.

*ewes

# GO AWAY LITTLE FAIRIES

*Hushaby, hushaby, go to sleep, go to sleep,*
*Hushaby, hushaby, go to sleep, my babe.*

*Go away, little fairies, go away, little fairies,*
*Go away little fairies, my babe must sleep.*

*Hushaby, hushaby, go to sleep, go to sleep,*
*Hushaby, hushaby, go to sleep, my babe.*

Watch o'er him, blessed angels,
　　watch o'er him, blessed angels,
Watch o'er him, blessed angels,
　　my babe will sleep.

# THE GARTAN MOTHER'S LULLABY

*Sleep, O babe for the red bee hums,*
*the silent twilight fall,*
*Sheevra from the grey rock comes to*
*wrap the world in thrall.*
*M'le anabh thu, my child, my joy,*
*my love and heart's desire,*
*The crickets sing you lullaby beside*
*the dying fire.*

# GOLDEN CRADLE

*Sweet babe, a golden cradle holds thee,*
*Soft snow white fleece enfolds thee,*
*Fairest flow'r are strewn before thee,*
*Sweet birds warble o'er thee.*
*Shoheen Sholo!*
*Lu, Lu, Lo, Lo!*

The Lullaby Songbook

TRACK 14

TRACK 15

# DANCE TO YOUR DADDY

*Dance to your daddy, my little laddie,*
*Dance to your daddy, my little man.*

*You shall have a fishy in your little dishy,*
*You shall have a fishy when the boat comes in.*

*Dance to your daddy, my little laddie,*
*Dance to your daddy, my little man.*

*You shall have a coaty, and a pair of britches,*
*You shall have a coaty when the boat comes in.*

**DANCE TO YOUR DADDY**

Dance to your daddy, my little laddie,
Dance to your daddy, my little man.

When you are a man and come to take a wife,
You shall wed a lass and love her all your life.

# GOLDEN SLUMBERS

Golden slumbers kiss your eyes,
Smiles await you when you rise,
Sleep pretty baby, do not cry,
And I will sing a lullaby.

Care you know not, therefore sleep,
While I o'er you watch do keep,
Sleep pretty baby, do not cry,
And I will sing a lullaby.

# HEY DIDDLE DIDDLE

*Hey diddle diddle, the cat and the fiddle,*
*The cow jumped over the moon,*
*The little dog laughed to see such fun,*
*And the dish ran away with the spoon.*

# EVENING HYMN

*Hear us, Father, as we pray,*
*Thou hast kept us through the day.*
*Fold us now in drowsy night,*
*Wake us with Thy morning light.*

TRACK 19

# HUSH LITTLE BABY

*Hush, little baby, don't say a word.*
*Papa's gonna buy you a mockingbird.*

*If that mockingbird won't sing,*
*Papa's gonna buy you a diamond ring.*

And if that diamond ring turns brass,
Papa's gonna buy you a looking glass.

And if that looking glass gets broke,
Papa's gonna buy you a billy goat.

And if that billy goat won't pull,
Papa's gonna buy you a cart and bull.

And if that cart and bull turn over,
Papa's gonna buy you a dog named Rover.

And if that dog named Rover won't bark
Papa's gonna buy you a horse and cart.


And if that horse and cart fall down,
You'll still be the sweetest little baby in town.

# HUSH-A-BYE, BABY

*Hush-a-bye, baby, on the tree top,*
*When the wind blows the cradle will rock.*
*When the bough breaks the cradle will fall,*
*Down will come baby, cradle and all.*

# LAVENDER'S BLUE

*Lavender's Blue, dilly dilly,*
*Lavender's green.*
*When I am King, dilly dilly,*
*You shall be Queen.*

Who told you so, dilly dilly,
Who told you so?
'Twas my own heart, dilly dilly,
That told me so.

**LAVENDER'S BLUE**

Call up your friends, dilly dilly,
Set them to work.
Some to the plough, dilly dilly,
Some to the fork.

Some to the hay, dilly dilly,
Some to thresh corn.
Whilst you and I, dilly dilly,
Keep ourselves warm.

*Lavender's Blue, dilly dilly,*
*Lavender's green.*
**When you are King, dilly dilly,**
*I shall be Queen.*

Who told you so, dilly dilly,
Who told you so?
'Twas my own heart, dilly dilly,
That told me so.

# O HUSH THEE, MY BABY

*O hush thee, my baby, thy sire is a knight,*
*Thy mother a lady, both lovely and bright.*
*The woods and the glens from*
*the towers which we see;*
*They all are belonging, dear baby to thee.*

O fear not the bugle,
  though loudly it blows,
It calls but the wardens that guard thy repose;
Their bows would be bended,
  their blades would be red,
Ere the step of a foeman draws near to thy bed.

**O HUSH THEE, MY BABY**

O hush thee, oh baby,
    the time soon will come,
When thy sleep be broken
    by trumpet and drum,
Then hush thee, my darling,
    take rest while you may,
For strife comes with manhood,
    and waking with day.

# LITTLE BO-PEEP

TRACK 23

Little Bo-Peep has lost her sheep,
And doesn't know where to find them.
Leave them alone and they'll come home,
Bringing their tails behind them.

Little Bo-Peep fell fast asleep,
And dreamed she heard them bleating.
But when she awoke,
she found it a joke,
For they were still a-fleeting.

Then up she took her little crook,
Determined for to find them.
She found them indeed,
but it made her heart bleed,
For they'd left their tails behind them.

# LAMBS ARE SLEEPING

Lullaby, oh, lullaby,
Flow'rs are closed and lambs are sleeping
Stars are up, the moon is peeping,
Lullaby, oh, lullaby.

While the birds are silence keeping,
Sleep, my baby fall asleeping.
Lullaby, oh, lullaby,
Lullaby, oh, lullaby.

# ROCK THE CRADLE

*Bye low, bye low,*
*Baby's in the cradle sleeping,*
*Tip toe, tip toe,*
*Still as pussy slyly creeping,*
*Bye low, bye low,*
*Rock the cradle, baby's waking,*
*Hush my baby, oh!*

TRACK 26

# LITTLE CHILDREN

Little children, tiny children,
So tired and so sleepy.
Weary children, drowsy children,
To dreamland will go.

In their bed with downy pillows,
The children's heads rest on.
Sleepy children, weary children,
To dreamland have gone.

# MANX LULLABY

O hush thee, my dove,
   O hush thee, my rowan,
O hush thee, my lapwing,
   my little brown bird.
O hush thee, my dove,
   O hush thee, my rowan,
O hush thee, my lapwing,
   my little brown bird.

# MANX LULLABY

O fold thy wing and seek thy nest now,
O shine the berry on the bright tree,
The bird is home from the mountain and valley,
O hush thee, my birdie, my pretty dearie.

O hush thee, my dove,
  O hush thee, my rowan,
O hush thee, my lapwing,
  my little brown bird.

# SLEEP ON, LITTLE ONE

*The flow'rets all sleep soundly,*
*Beneath the moon's bright ray,*
*They nod their heads together,*
*And dream the night away.*

*The budding trees wave to and fro,*
*And murmur soft and low.*
*Sleep on! Sleep on,*
*Sleep on, my little one!*

# SLEEP, BABY, SLEEP

Sleep, baby, sleep,
Your daddy's tending the sheep,
Your mummy's taken the cows away,
And won't be home 'til the break of day.
Sleep, baby, sleep.

Sleep, baby, sleep,
Our cottage vale is deep,
The little lamb is on the green,
With snowy fleece so soft and clean,
Sleep, baby, sleep.

# SLEEP, LITTLE CHILD

*Sleep, little child, go to sleep,*
*Mother is here by thy bed.*
*Sleep, little child, go to sleep,*
*Rest on thy pillow thy head.*

*The word is silent and still;*
*The moon shines bright on the hill,*
*And creeps past thy window sill,*
*Sleep, little child, go to sleep,*
*Oh, sleep, go to sleep.*

# ROCK-A-BYE-BABY

*Rockabye, baby, on the treetop,*
*When the wind blows, the cradle will rock,*
*When the bough breaks, the cradle will fall,*
*And down will come baby, cradle and all.*

TRACK 32

# SLEEPYTIME

*Sleepytime has come for my baby.*
*Baby now is going to sleep.*
*Kiss mama goodnight and we'll turn out the light,*
*While I tuck you in bed, 'neath your covers tight.*
*Sleepytime has come for my baby.*
*Baby now is going to sleep.*

# SWEET AND LOW

*Sweet and low, sweet and low,*
*Wind of the western sea,*
*Low, low, breathe and blow,*
*Wind of the western sea,*
*Over the rolling waters go,*
*Come from the dying moon and blow,*
*Blow him again to me,*
*While my little one,*
    *while my pretty one, sleeps.*

## SWEET AND LOW

*Sleep and rest, sleep and rest,*
*Father will come to thee soon,*
*Rest, rest on mother's breast,*
*Father will come to thee soon.*

Father will come to his babe in the nest,
Silver sails all out of the west,
Under the silver moon,
Sleep, my little one, sleep my pretty one, sleep.

# TEDDY BEAR, TEDDY BEAR

*Teddy Bear, Teddy Bear, turn around,*
*Teddy Bear, Teddy Bear, touch the ground.*
*Teddy Bear, Teddy Bear, show your shoe,*
*Teddy Bear, Teddy Bear, I love you.*

*Teddy Bear, Teddy Bear, climb the stairs,*
*Teddy Bear, Teddy Bear, say your prayers.*
*Teddy Bear, Teddy Bear, turn off the light,*
*Teddy Bear, Teddy Bear, say goodnight.*

# WEE WILLIE WINKIE

TRACK 35

Wee Willie Winkie
Runs through the town,
Upstairs and downstairs
In his nightgown.

Rapping at the windows,
Crying through the lock,
'Are the children all in bed?
For it's now eight o'clock.'

# TWINKLE, TWINKLE, LITTLE STAR

*Twinkle, twinkle, little star*
*How I wonder what you are!*
*Up above the world so high*
*Like a diamond in the sky,*
*Twinkle, twinkle, little star*
*How I wonder what you are.*

# WINKUM, WINKUM

*Winkum, winkum, shut your eye,*
*Sweet, my baby, lullaby,*
*For the dews are falling soft,*
*Light are flick'ring up aloft.*
*And the moonlight's peeping over,*
*Yonder hilltop capped with clover.*

Chickens long have gone to rest,
Birds lie snug within their nest,
And my birdie soon will be
Sleeping like a chickadee.
For with only half a try,
Winkum, winkum shuts her eye.

**WINKUM, WINKUM**